Jalaine

MW01028027

Zack, You're Acting Zany!

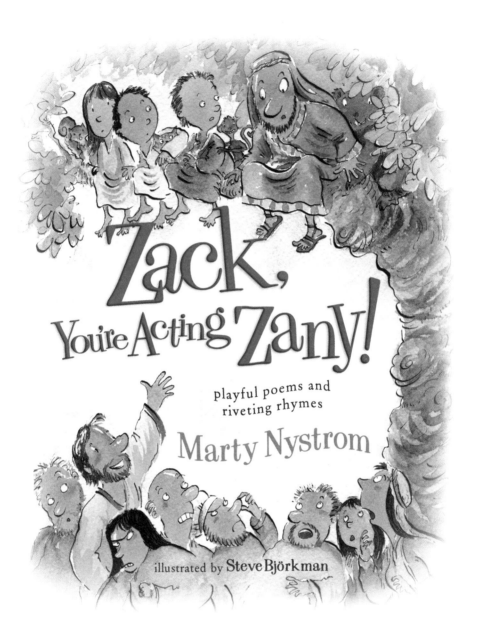

Zack, You're Acting Zany!

playful poems and
riveting rhymes

Marty Nystrom

illustrated by Steve Björkman

Standard®
PUBLISHING

Cincinnati, Ohio

Published by Standard Publishing, Cincinnati, Ohio
www.standardpub.com

Printed in: China
Project editor: Diane Stortz
Jacket and interior design: The DesignWorks Group, Jason Gabbert

ISBN 978-0-7847-2193-3

Library of Congress Cataloging-in-Publication Data

Nystrom, Marty.
  Zack, you're acting zany! : playful poems and riveting
rhymes / Marty Nystrom ; illustrated by Steve Björkman.
     p. cm.
  Includes index.
  ISBN 978-0-7847-2193-3 (casebound with jacket)
  1. Bible--Juvenile poetry. 2. Children's poetry,
American. 3. Humorous poetry, American. I. Björkman,
Steve. II. Title.
  PS3614.Y7Z33 2010
  811'.6--dc22
                        2009037634

16 15 14 13 12 11 10   9 8 7 6 5 4 3 2 1

To my sons, Nathan and Benjamin.

Marty

For the wild and crazy Schulz family!

Steve

Contents

Acknowledgements

Thank you to my writing group for your encouragement and expertise: Judy Bodmer, Thorn Ford, Betsy Hernandez, Peg Kehle, Kathy Kohler, Kate Lloyd, and Paul Malm. Thanks also to Geoff and Lynn Lyon for hosting us every Thursday morning at The Lyon's Den.

Thank you to our home group, especially leaders Bill and Marlene Brubaker, for your constant and visionary prayer support. Thank you to the Murfitt family for your priceless friendship and for allowing me to share some of Gabe's story.

Thank you, Diane Stortz and Standard Publishing, for your pursuit of excellence.

Thanks to my parents, Don and Elajean Nystrom, and to seven of the funniest people I know, my siblings: Maribeth, David, Donela, Lynne, Julie, Sarah, and Lisa.

Thanks, Nate and Ben. It's been a blast watching you grow up. Thanks always to my beautiful wife, Jeanne. Your sense of humor refreshes many.

Introduction

I was an elementary school teacher. The kids in my class loved it when I read funny poetry aloud. Their response was always, "Read another one, Mr. Nystrom! Please!" Many of these crazy poems had valuable lessons woven into their rhyme and humor. Laughter and learning worked hand in hand.

Jesus was a captivating storyteller. His colorful parables grabbed the attention of his listeners and taught important truths. Some of his tales had a comical predicament or a surprise ending. He even exaggerated sometimes to get his point across. He talked about a man with a log in his eye and a camel squeezing through the hole in a needle.

Jesus met a lot of amusing characters too. You don't have to look hard to find funny situations in the New Testament!

I hope this book will make you laugh and want to look into God's wonderful Word yourself to learn more!

Gospel Singers

Matthew sings the tenor part.
Mark's on melody.
Luke belts out the baritone,
and John sings bass with glee.

We sing about the good news
of One you won't forget.
We're Matthew, Mark, Luke, and John—
the original gospel quartet!

Charades

Poor ol' Zachariah!
He cannot speak a word.
He's trying hard to tell us
what he saw and what he heard.
He flaps his arms
like outstretched wings—
it really looks absurd!
Why's the guy so tongue-tied
just because he saw a bird?

What did Zachariah see and hear?
Find out in Luke 1.

O Miss Mary

O Miss Mary,
it must have been so scary
when the angel
just appeared outside your door.

O Miss Mary,
it had to be quite eerie—
for no angel
ever visited before.

O Miss Mary,
did it seem imaginary
as you trembled on your knees
down on the floor?

O Miss Mary,
weren't you sort of wary
when he told you
everything God had in store?

O Miss Mary,
it's so extraordinary—
you said yes to the message
that he bore.

O Miss Mary,
the baby that you carry
is the promised One
we've all been waiting for!

What did Mary tell the angel?
Look in Luke 1:38.

13

Johnny Jump Up

When John was in
his mother's tummy,
he would sometimes
jump for joy.
He was what
is often called
a bouncing baby boy.

When I was in
my mother's tummy,
I would sometimes
kick my heels.
So when my mom
reads this story,
she says,
"I know how that feels!"

Why did John jump?
Read Luke 1:39-45.

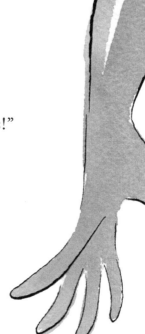

14

Donkey Work

Clip, clop, clip, clop.
Keep on stepping. Cannot stop.
Three days yet
until we get
to Bethlehem.

Clip, clop, clip, clop.
Weary Mary rides up top.
Two days yet
until we get
to Bethlehem.

Clip, clop, clip, clop.
Hope poor Joseph doesn't drop.
One day yet
until we get
to Bethlehem.

Clip, clop, clip, clop.
Almost there. It's just a hop.
Soon they will
be mom and pop
in Bethlehem.

Clip, clop, clip, clop.
A bed of straw. I go *ker-plop.*
Feels so good
to finally stop
in Bethlehem!

What was this trip about?
Read Luke 2:1-5.

Swaddling Clothes

The Bible says
that Mary wrapped
her babe in swaddling clothes—
strips of cloth
wound 'round and 'round
his shoulders to his toes.
This makes me think of Christmas gifts
kids often get from grandmas,
but we don't call 'em swaddling clothes—
we call 'em striped pajamas.

She brought forth her firstborn son, and wrapped him in swaddling clothes.—Luke 2:7, KJV

Humble Beginnings

"Were you born in a barn?"
my father often shouts
when I slurp my soup
or burp at the table.
But I don't get all flustered
or get my feelings hurt,
'cause even baby Jesus
was born in a stable!

Stable Talk

"*Hee haw*'s been born!
Hee haw's been born!"
the shaggy donkey brays.

"Oh, thank you, Lord,
for the *tweet* baby boy,"
the tiny sparrow prays.

20

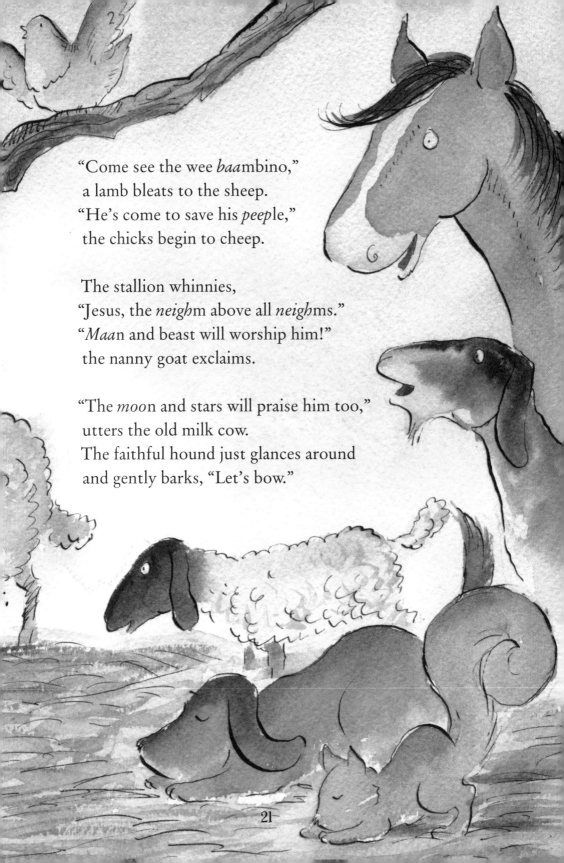

"Come see the wee *baa*mbino,"
a lamb bleats to the sheep.
"He's come to save his *peep*le,"
the chicks begin to cheep.

The stallion whinnies,
"Jesus, the *neigh*m above all *neigh*ms."
"*Maa*n and beast will worship him!"
the nanny goat exclaims.

"The *moo*n and stars will praise him too,"
utters the old milk cow.
The faithful hound just glances around
and gently barks, "Let's bow."

21

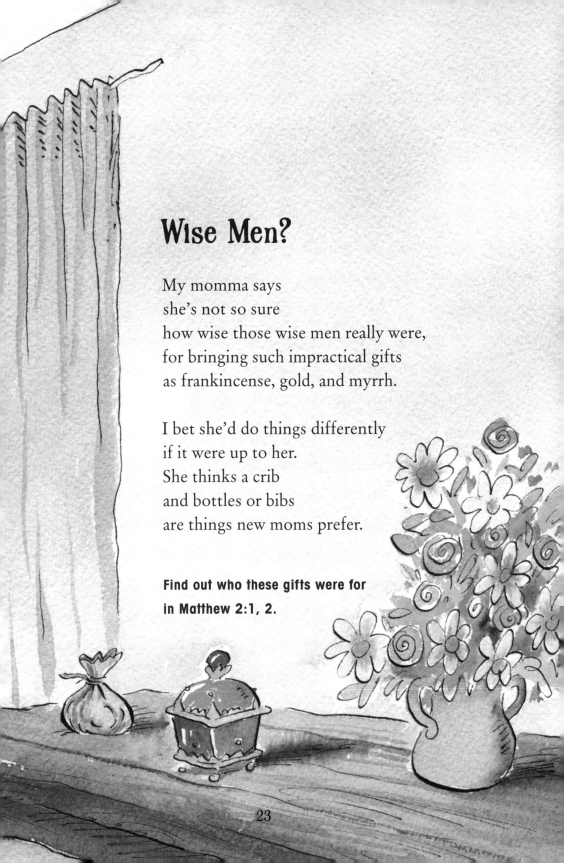

Wise Men?

My momma says
she's not so sure
how wise those wise men really were,
for bringing such impractical gifts
as frankincense, gold, and myrrh.

I bet she'd do things differently
if it were up to her.
She thinks a crib
and bottles or bibs
are things new moms prefer.

**Find out who these gifts were for
in Matthew 2:1, 2.**

Christmas Play

Peter was picked to play the part
of wise man number two,
but his mother just phoned to say he is home,
lying flat on his back with the flu.

Mrs. Hector, our drama director,
shouted with worry and shock,
"Our Christmas play is an hour away!
Curtain's at two o'clock!

"We must do something quickly!
We have to find somebody fast!
But I've already used every boy in our room
to fill all the parts in the cast.

"Jamal is starring as Joseph.
The innkeeper's played by Ken.
Fernando's the front of the donkey,
and Billy is billed as 'back end.'

"Shiko and Shane are the shepherds.
Ben, Brad, and Brett are their beasts.
Kevin and Kwan are the other two boys
who are playing the kings from the East."

Well, I knew that I had the answer.
It was plain as the nose on my face.
So, willing to help, I suggested myself
to perform in Peter's place.

Mrs. Hector thought for a second.
Then she shouted, "Let's give it a whirl!
I'm sure it's fine—the Lord won't mind
if our story has one wise GIRL."

Open Invitation

The wise men are rolling in money.
The shepherds are just flat broke.

The wise men are regal and kingly.
The shepherds are just common folk.

The wise men are schooled and cultured.
The shepherds are hillbilly hicks.

The wise men were raised in great castles.
The shepherds grew up in the sticks.

You might be a wise man,
you might be a shepherd,
or somebody in-between.

It doesn't matter—
you're invited to come
and worship the newborn king.

"I bring you good news
that will bring great joy
to all people."—Luke 2:10

Herod's Gone a-Huntin'

King Herod's gone a-huntin'—
he's searchin' everywhere.
He doesn't stalk a deer or fox,
a lion or a hare.
You're safe if you're a bobcat,
a buffalo or bear,
but if you are a baby boy . . .
you'd better just beware!

Why was King Herod so mean?
Read Matthew 2:16.

27

God Became a Baby Boy

It's pretty hard to picture,
but according to the Scripture,
God became a bitty baby boy.
Whoever could imagine
he would leave his throne in Heaven
and become a waddlin' toddler
with a bottle and a toy?

The maker of the universe,
creator of the sun and earth,
the mighty one who made the mountains quake,
once loved to sit and squeal and laugh
while splashing in a bubble bath
or playing peekaboo and pat-a-cake.

The one who authored time and space
and put the planets in their place,
who had the endless galaxies arranged,
once needed to be dressed and fed
and burped and rocked and put to bed
and even have his dirty diaper changed.

It truly is astonishing,
amazing as can be,
that God was once a tiny baby,
just like you and me!

"Before Abraham was even born, I AM!"
—John 8:58

30

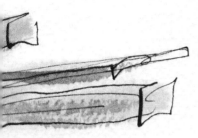

The Carpenter's Son

My father is a carpenter.
He sure knows how to build!
He carves and cuts and works with wood—
his hands are truly skilled.
I get to work beside my dad
so I can learn the trade.
I watch him closely every day
to learn how things are made.
Like tables and chairs, barrels and shelves,
and boats of every size—
it's like he's working miracles
right there before my eyes!
Someday when I am older,
I hope to be that good.
Perhaps I'll work a wonder too,
with nails and beams of wood.

Amazing!

Awesome!
Astounding!
A wonder to behold!

Remarkable!
Astonishing!
So confident and bold!

Brilliant!
Phenomenal!
And such a heart of gold!

But what is most amazing...
he's only twelve years old!

Who was this wise young man?
Find out in Luke 2:41-47.

Lost and Found

I got lost at the county fair.
Poor Ma and Pa got quite a scare!
But soon they found me sittin' there,
eatin' cotton candy on the bleachers.

Mary and Joseph had a scare.
They looked for Jesus everywhere!
They finally found him sittin' there,
talkin' with the elders and the teachers.

My ma and pa were sure upset
when I got left behind,
but Jesus' parents thought they'd lost
the Savior of mankind!

Locusts for Lunch

It's gross enough
that John the Baptist
gobbled up grasshoppers.
But here's what makes it even worse—
the kind he chomped were whoppers!

Read Mark 1:6 to find out what else John ate.

Announcers

My uncle's the announcer
at a Little League park.
He tells the fans who's comin' up to bat.
He shouts, "This kid's a slugger!
He's hitting like Babe Ruth!"
and other big important stuff like that.

My grandpa's the announcer
on a radio show.
He introduces all the special guests.
He says, "Don't turn your dial!
We're gonna be right back!
I promise—you don't want to miss the rest."

John was the announcer
of the world's greatest news.
He told the crowds, "The Lord is on his way!"
He cried, "Get ready, people!
It's time to turn from sin!
Obey the Lord, and be baptized today!"

What prophet wrote about John?
Look in Mark 1:1, 2.

Nicodemus's Dilemma

My mama, she done taught me right.
She didn't raise no dummy.
I know I can't go back and be
a baby in her tummy.
I have been a grown-up now
since goodness-who-knows-when.
So why did Jesus say to me,
"You must be born again"?

What else did Jesus tell Nicodemus?
Read John 3:16.

Titanic Catch

Help! Help! We're sinking!
Our boat is going down!
We didn't slam an iceberg,
ram a reef,
or run aground—
we're in this grim predicament
because we got our wish.
Help! Help! We're sinking!
We caught too many fish!

Read this story in Luke 5:5-7.

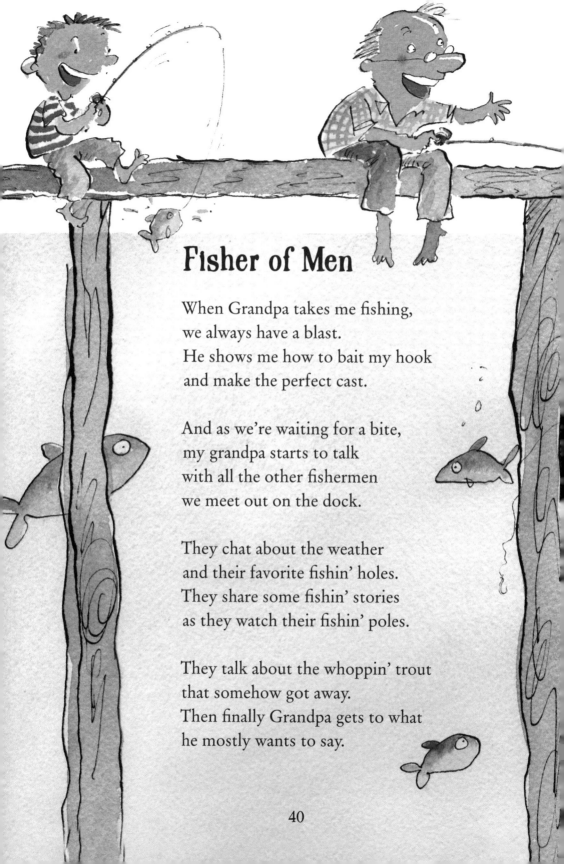

Fisher of Men

When Grandpa takes me fishing,
we always have a blast.
He shows me how to bait my hook
and make the perfect cast.

And as we're waiting for a bite,
my grandpa starts to talk
with all the other fishermen
we meet out on the dock.

They chat about the weather
and their favorite fishin' holes.
They share some fishin' stories
as they watch their fishin' poles.

They talk about the whoppin' trout
that somehow got away.
Then finally Grandpa gets to what
he mostly wants to say.

He tells 'em, "Jesus changed my life
and washed away my sin."
He says, "I haven't been the same
since I was born again!"

And while he's testifyin'
and I'm pulling in a perch,
I hear ol' Gramps invitin'
all those fishermen to church.

Poor Grandpa rarely hooks a fish—
he doesn't watch his rod.
But one thing that he's awesome at
is catching men for God!

"I will show you how to fish for people!"
—Mark 1:17

Up on the Housetop

Be careful! Be steady!
Don't stumble! Don't goof!
It's very, very scary
to be carried on a roof.
No clowning! No horseplay!
Don't tease me! Don't spoof!
Remember, you all promised me
your plan is foolproof.

Why was this man on the roof?
Read Mark 2:2-4.

43

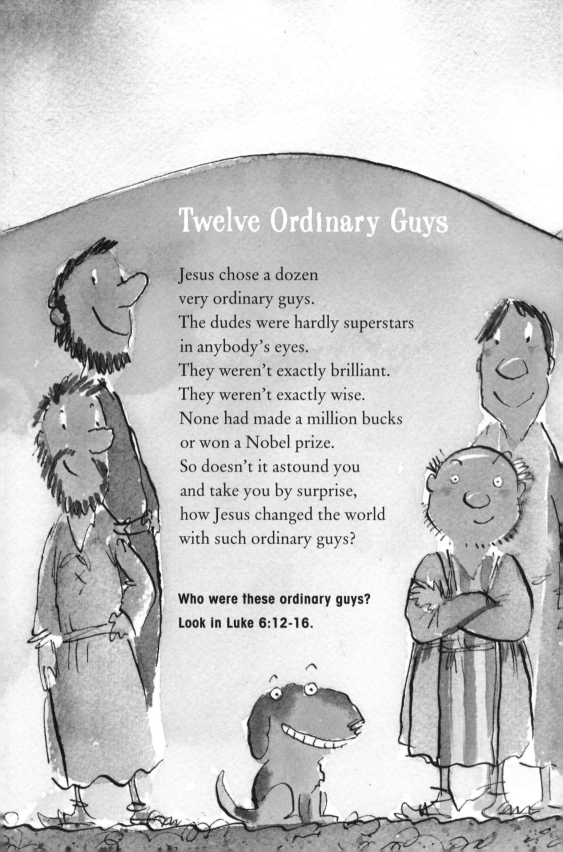

Twelve Ordinary Guys

Jesus chose a dozen
very ordinary guys.
The dudes were hardly superstars
in anybody's eyes.
They weren't exactly brilliant.
They weren't exactly wise.
None had made a million bucks
or won a Nobel prize.
So doesn't it astound you
and take you by surprise,
how Jesus changed the world
with such ordinary guys?

Who were these ordinary guys?
Look in Luke 6:12-16.

Mountaintop Experience

Jesus preached a sermon on a mountain.
Folks climbed up the rocky slope
to hear him share good news.
So if you plan to hear this mighty preacher,
just be sure to wear a pair
of sturdy hiking shoes!

**His disciples gathered around him, and he
began to teach.—Matthew 5:1, 2**

Miss Giver

Is everybody watching?
Can everybody see?
I'll wait to drop my offering in
when every eye's on me.
Would someone blow a trumpet now?
A fanfare would be great!
But not too loud—the crowd must hear
my pennies *plink* the plate.

It feels so good to give to God.
It fills my heart with cheer.
And that is why
I just can't wait
to give again—
next year.

What reward will this giver get?
Read Matthew 6:2.

Salt of the Earth

Popcorn without salt is blah and boring.
Pretzels without salt are blecchy and bland.
Salt-free French fries start my taste buds snoring.
Saltless grits taste just like gritty sand.

Salt is the thing that puts zing into crackers.
Salt gives the zest to crisp tater chips.
If there were no salt, there'd be plenty of snackers
who wouldn't be licking or smacking their lips.

In Matthew 5:13 I read
the purpose for my birth:
there Jesus says that I should be
like salt to this ol' earth.

49

Night-Light

My momma bought a night-light
to plug into the wall,
so I can find the bathroom
at the far end of the hall.

Before she got that night-light,
I couldn't see at all.
I'd stumble in the darkness
and sometimes trip and fall.

Thank goodness for that night-light,
for though it's pretty small,
it lets me make a beeline
when I answer nature's call.

Lord, let me be a night-light—
let all I say and do
help people in the darkness
find the way that leads to you.

"Let your good deeds shine out."
—Matthew 5:16

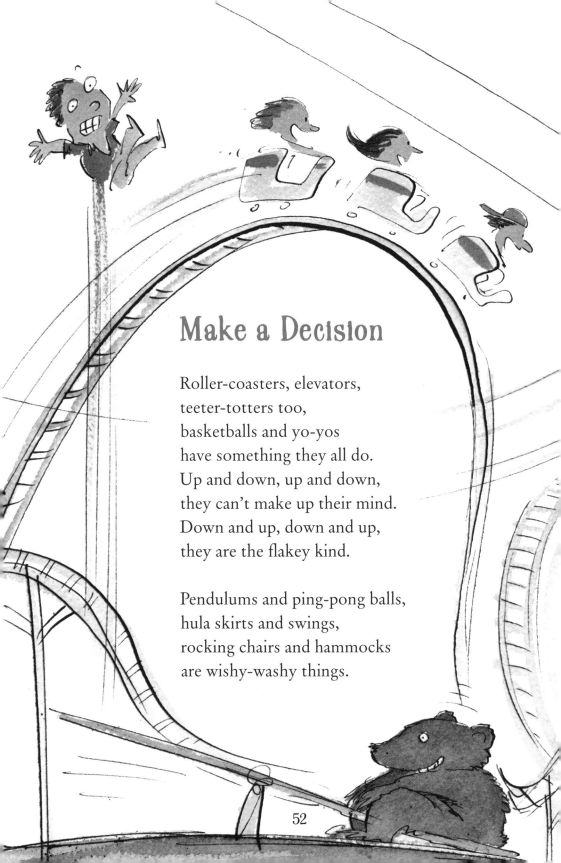

Make a Decision

Roller-coasters, elevators,
teeter-totters too,
basketballs and yo-yos
have something they all do.
Up and down, up and down,
they can't make up their mind.
Down and up, down and up,
they are the flakey kind.

Pendulums and ping-pong balls,
hula skirts and swings,
rocking chairs and hammocks
are wishy-washy things.

Back and forth, back and forth,
they can't make up their mind.
Forth and back, forth and back,
they are the flakey kind.

A boomerang cannot decide
if it should come or go,
but I will let my yes be yes
and let my no be no!

"Just say a simple, 'Yes, I will,' or 'No, I won't.'"
—Matthew 5:37

Proud Pray-er

I'm Mrs. Pridella Vainetta von Kay.
I'm sure you can tell that I love to pray.
I start in the morning and go all day,
because I have so much to say.
I stand on the corner of First and Main
(unless it looks like it could rain).
I proudly pray, so loud and clear,
whenever crowds of people appear.
(I only pray if someone's near—
what good is a prayer
that no one can hear?)

Who loves to pray just to be seen?
Look in Matthew 6:5.

Safekeeping

My favorite sweater
now looks like Swiss cheese.
A moth in my closet
destroyed it with ease.

My speedy red scooter
has bitten the dust.
It sat out all winter—
it's nothin' but rust.

My basketball sneakers
with black-and-gold trim
were stolen last Saturday
down at the gym.

Protecting my treasures
can truly be tough.
There must be a safe place
to store all my stuff!

**Find the best place to store treasures.
Read Matthew 6:20.**

Bird Food

Swallows swallow skeeters
as they flitter through the sky.
Pigeons peck at popcorn in the park.
Herons hog up polliwogs
as they go wrigglin' by.
Owls chow on critters in the dark.
Chickens feed on chicken feed,
chickadees eat teeny seeds,
and fruit is what a toucan's loopy for.
Turkeys gobble gobs of grain,
ducks find dinner in the rain,
and seagulls nosh on sushi
that has washed up on the shore.
Pelicans and penguins
really relish smelly fish.

Robins slurp up squirmy worms
and find them quite delish.
A spicy snack of rattlesnake
is what roadrunners wish,
and even rotten roadkill
is a buzzard's favorite dish.

If God feeds all his feathered friends
with snakes and seeds and squid,
I know that he'll take of me,
because I am his kid!

**Read what Jesus said about this in
Matthew 6:26.**

Get me
outta here!

First Things First

My cart won't get to market
if you sit there on your tush.
You haven't moved a muscle.
Don't you know you're s'posed to push?
Aha! I see the problem.
It's simple! Well, of course!
I'll tell you what the matter is—
I need a smarter horse!

This empty-headed farmer
had the order out of whack.
He should have had the horse in front
and put the cart in back.

Oh Lord, please help me live my life
so things aren't all reversed.
I really want to get it right
and always put you first!

**"Seek first his kingdom and his righteousness."
—Matthew 6:33, NIV**

Joe Judgmental

Hello, I'm Joe Judgmental!
I want to be your friend.
My words are frank but gentle.
I'm sure they won't offend.
I'll give you my opinion
to point out all your sin.
Please give me full attention.
I'm ready to begin:
Don't you think your shaggy hair
is just a bit too long?
Your underarm deodorant
smells just a tad too strong?

And did I see you swaying
to the rhythm of this song?
Good thing I'm here to set you straight
and show you where you're wrong.
Your paunch is lookin' pudgy,
like you ate a ton of fudge.
And when it's time to exercise,
I bet you barely budge.

I sense that you are furious—
but you shouldn't hold a grudge.
I think you should be thankful
that you have me for a judge!

**"Do not judge others, and you will not
be judged."—Matthew 7:1**

Speck-tator

What's that little speck I spy,
that teeny spot on your right eye?
Is it grime? Is it slime?
Or is that tiny fleck a fly?

I also see a glob of goop.
It's yellowish green, like split pea soup.
The icky goo is thick as glue
   and makes your eyelid sorta droop.

   And on your lash is just a hint
   of fuzzy-wuzzy laundry lint.
I bet that's why you rub your eye
and always wink and squint.

As long as I am on a roll,
I'll carry on with speck patrol.
I think your—
What's that, you ask?
What's in *my* eye?
Oh that—it's just a ten-foot pole.

"First get rid of the log in your own eye."
—Luke 6:42

Snake Sandwich

If I asked Dad for a PB and J,
my pop would make it the proper way.
He wouldn't serve a rattlesnake
between two rocks, for heaven's sake!
(Unless, of course, it's April Fool's Day.)

Who gives the best gifts? See Matthew 7:11.

Which Way?

Here I stand at a fork in the road,
just scratchin' and scratchin' my head.
Should I take that big, broad street
or this narrow path instead?

That way's flat and easy.
I could walk it in my sleep.
This way's high and hilly.
It's so rocky, rough, and steep.

This way? That way?
That way? This way?
Which way should I choose?
Tell me, which road you would take
if you were in my shoes?

**"You can enter God's Kingdom only through the
narrow gate."—Matthew 7:13**

Sham Lamb

Don't attempt to pet a sheep
until you check it out.
First inspect its legs and feet
and then its teeth and snout.

Does it have large wolfy paws
with lots of sharp and wolfy claws?
Does it have long wolfy fangs
that hang from strong and wolfy jaws?
Does the creature sweetly bleat,
or does it sorta growl?
And when it sees the moon above,
does it begin to howl?
Well, if it does, its fleeciness
is surely just skin deep.
I recommend you flee from there—
I'm sure it's not a sheep.

Who comes disguised as harmless sheep?
Look in Matthew 7:15.

Card Castle

My castle was colossal.
My castle was complex.
I built it out of playing cards
from sixty-seven decks.

But then my grand creation
was destroyed in just a flash—
it had a weak foundation
and collapsed with one big *crash*.

My castle was colossal,
the best you've ever seen.
(But next time I won't build it
on our neighbor's trampoline.)

Want to build a good life?
Check out Matthew 7:24.

Hog Haven

The pig that built a straw house
and the pig that built with sticks
are like the foolish guy
in Matthew 7:26.
He built his house on shifting sand.
He should have built on solid land.
His shaky shanty couldn't stand,
and he was in a fix.

The pig that built his sturdy house
completely out of bricks
just chuckled at the big bad wolf
and all his dirty tricks.
His huffs and puffs were not enough
to blow down piggy's door—
that clever hog had studied
Matthew 7:24.

Be Still

My teacher often says, "Be still!"
and yet I twist and squirm.
I squiggle and I wriggle
and I wiggle like a worm.

I s'pose that I should try to be
more like the wind and waves—
whenever Jesus says, "Be still!"
the weather just behaves.

Read this story in Matthew 8:23-27.

Head Count

I understand how God can count
the hairs on Grandpa's head,
but just how does
he number the fuzz
on frizzy cousin Fred?

**"The very hairs on your head are
all numbered."—Matthew 10:30**

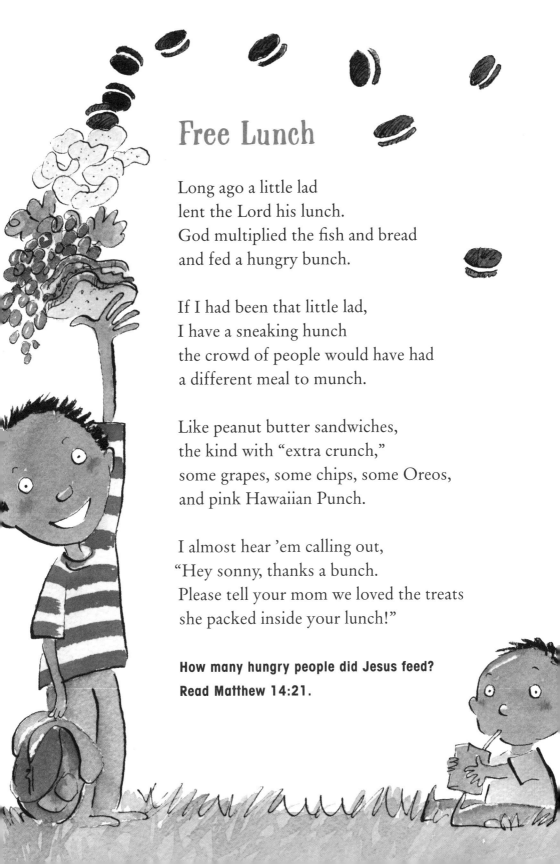

Free Lunch

Long ago a little lad
lent the Lord his lunch.
God multiplied the fish and bread
and fed a hungry bunch.

If I had been that little lad,
I have a sneaking hunch
the crowd of people would have had
a different meal to munch.

Like peanut butter sandwiches,
the kind with "extra crunch,"
some grapes, some chips, some Oreos,
and pink Hawaiian Punch.

I almost hear 'em calling out,
"Hey sonny, thanks a bunch.
Please tell your mom we loved the treats
she packed inside your lunch!"

How many hungry people did Jesus feed?
Read Matthew 14:21.

I Pity Poor Ol' Peter

I pity poor ol' Peter,
who tried to walk on water.
He took a step
then sank into the sea.

See ya, Pete!

Even I did better—
I stayed up on the water.
(Of course it helps
to have a water ski!)

Why did Peter sink?
Look in Matthew 14:30.

Bread of Life

Dwight likes white.
Pete likes wheat.
Anita says that pita
is her favorite bread to eat.
Ty likes rye.
Dan likes bran.
Maria says tortillas
are a *mucho bueno* treat.
And even picky eater
skinny Dieter von Hoff
loves pumpernickel toast
with the crusts cut off.

Bread is so delicious!
It's yummy as can be.
It also is nutritious,
and it gives us energy.
Jesus said, "I am the bread"
in John 6:35,
'cause Jesus feeds our spirits,
and he keeps our souls alive.

Saliva Salve

Good thing I didn't throw a fit.
Good thing I didn't holler "QUIT!"
or get into a silly snit
and let my temper rise.
Good thing I didn't turn and split.
Good thing I didn't mind one bit
when Jesus used a gob of spit
to heal my blinded eyes!

Where did this happen?
Look in Mark 8:22-25.

78

Hotdog Seeds?

Jesus spoke of mustard seeds,
and what he said was true.
So are there seeds for ketchup
and for pickle relish too?

What did Jesus compare to a mustard seed?
Look in Matthew 17:20.

Role Reversal

Mother tells me, "Be a lady."
Father tells me, "Be mature."
Grandma says I gotta grow up,
settle down, and act like her.

Kids like me should not be sassy,
so I will not cause a fuss—
but didn't Jesus tell the grown-ups
they're supposed to be like us?

What did Jesus tell the grown-ups?
Look in Matthew 18:3.

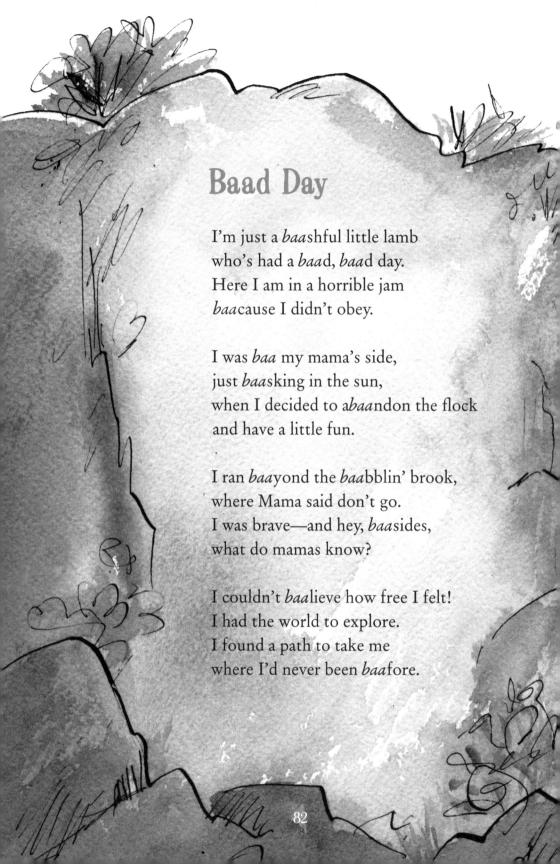

Baad Day

I'm just a *baa*shful little lamb
who's had a *baa*d, *baa*d day.
Here I am in a horrible jam
*baa*cause I didn't obey.

I was *baa* my mama's side,
just *baa*sking in the sun,
when I decided to a*baa*ndon the flock
and have a little fun.

I ran *baa*yond the *baa*bblin' brook,
where Mama said don't go.
I was brave—and hey, *baa*sides,
what do mamas know?

I couldn't *baa*lieve how free I felt!
I had the world to explore.
I found a path to take me
where I'd never been *baa*fore.

*Baa*ck and forth and up a *baa*nk,
I followed the twists and bends,
until I *baa*held the brink of a cliff
where the trail just suddenly ends.

But then I lost my *baa*lance
*baa*side the canyon's edge.
I tumbled like an acro*baa*t
and landed on this ledge.

Now my leg is all *baa*nged up—
I need a *baa*ndage baad.
My *baa*ck is sore; my *baa*hind hurts.
I'm feeling scared and sad.

I'm *baa*ffled at my *baa*havior.
I know that I was wrong.
Oh, how I want to be *baa*ck home,
'cause that's where I *baa*long!

**Will anyone help this *baa*d lamb
home again? Read Matthew 18:12-14.**

Counting Sheep

Ninety-one, ninety-two,
I'm almost through.
Ninety-three, ninety-four,
now just six more.
Ninety-five, ninety-six,
ninety-seven, ninety-eight,
ninety-nine, one hun—
Oh, no! Where's Nate?

You all stay here
where it's safe and warm.
I've got to go out
in the thunderstorm.
I'll search in the forest,
the fields, and the farms.
Then I'll be back
with Nate in my arms.

Math Problem

70 times 7?
All righty,
let's see . . .
70 times 7?
What would the answer be?
My brothers, they are triplets,
so I multiply by three.
Hmm . . .
I think it is one thousand and
four hundred seventy.

Of course, I have to calculate
my seven sisters too.
Phew! I have a mountain of
forgiving left to do!

**Read what Jesus taught about forgiveness
in Matthew 18:21, 22.**

Good Sam

Yesterday at recess
I fell down and cut my knee.
I hoped and prayed that someone
would come by and rescue me.

The first to stop was teacher's pet,
the prissy Meg McCludd.
But she just took off screaming,
"Yuck! I hate the sight of blood!"

And then I saw Josh coming—
the coolest jock in class.
But he just ran right by me
on his way to catch a pass.

So as I lay there hurting
and feeling awfully weak,
who should come to help me up?
A kid we call The Geek.

His name is really Samuel,
and he is pretty nerdy,
but as I hobbled to the nurse,
Sam's arm felt strong and sturdy.

My knee is in a bandage now.
I know that it will mend.
I'm kinda glad that I fell down—
I found an awesome friend.

**Read how Jesus told this story
in Luke 10:30-37.**

Martha's Complaint

Mary, Mary, quite contrary,
how can you sit on your duff?
There's work to do,
and I need you
to help with all this stuff:

There's wool to weave and beds to make,
fish to clean and bread to bake.
Lots of pots and plates to wash,
gobs and gobs of grapes to squash.
A tub to scrub, a floor to sweep—
  you know we've got a house to keep!
  There's meat to chop and fruit to peel
  before we stop to have a meal.
  Our Lord won't get a thing to eat
  if you just sit there at his feet.

  Oh, tell her, Jesus, how I feel!

What's that, Lord?
Could this be true?
You say my little sister found
a better thing to do?

**Read what Jesus told Martha
in Luke 10:42.**

Knock, Knock

Knock, knock. Who's there?
It's me, your neighbor—Mrs. O'Hare.
Some guests have come. My cupboard is bare.
Have you any food to spare?

     Mrs. O'Hare, I do declare!
It's 3 a.m.—are you aware?
Come back at 10.
  I know by then
    that I'll be more than glad to share.
 Good night, God bless you, Mrs. O'Hare.
Be safe, be warm, please do take care.

Knock, knock. Who's there?
It's me again, just Mrs. O'Hare.
I know it's late, but I can't wait.
I have a meal I must prepare.

    You listen here, oh Mrs. O'Hare!
    You woke us up—how do you dare?
      Your noise is more than I can bear!
     I still have curlers in my hair.
      My husband's in his underwear.
      It's dark and damp and cold out there!

Come back at 9. I'll find some bread.
Good night! I'm going back to bed.

Knock, knock! Knock, knock!
Ooh . . . I'll be right there.
I'm gettin' so sick
of this whole affair.
Just give me a minute.
Don't go anywhere.
I'll find you some food
in my old Frigidaire.
You sure are persistent,
oh Mrs. O'Hare!

Jesus said that we should be
more like this Mrs. O'Hare.
It's good to be persistent,
'specially when we go to prayer.

**Read how Jesus told this story
in Luke 11:5-10.**

The Pharisees Are Phurious

The Pharisees are phurious.
They're really phreakin' out.
They're phrantic and they're phlustered.
They're phoaming at the mouth.

What's got 'em in a phrenzy?
Why do they phume and spout?
Go look in Luke to phind out what
the phuss is all about.

What upset the Pharisees?
Read Luke 11:37, 38.

Bird's-Eye View

It's time to rest
up in my nest.
My tummy's full of seeds.
I never fret.
I don't forget
that God meets all my needs.

Those folks below
are on the go
with much too much to do.
They worry so—
don't people know
God cares about them too?

Who does God value more than the birds?
Read Luke 12:6, 7.

King Klifford

King Klifford was quite a collector.
He liked to accumulate things.
It brought him great pleasure
just knowing his treasure
was grander than all other kings'.

King Klifford was never contented—
he hadn't collected enough!
And so he kept filling
big barns and big buildings
by storing and stashing more stuff.

The king had a cave full of jewels
and fleets of the fanciest cars.
He owned lots of yachts,
rare porcelain pots,
and loads of electric guitars.

He stockpiled nickels and pennies
and bills filling millions of wallets.
He gathered great gobs
of new thingamabobs
and doodads and whatchamacallits.

He bought a whole bargeful of baseballs
and billions of beautiful beads.
He shopped for gold rings
and ordered more things
than anyone actually needs.
Like piles of pickleball paddles
and oodles of loud cuckoo clocks,
long limousines,
used washing machines,
and boxes and boxes of rocks.

Year after year he kept hoarding.
He never was quite satisfied.
'Til finally one day,
while shopping away,
King Klifford keeled over and died.

King Klifford was never contented.
His story's so sorry and sad.
With treasures galore,
he just wanted more—
but never enjoyed what he had.

**Read what Jesus taught about possessions
in Luke 12:15.**

95

Flower Show

Roses in red satin,
magnolias all in white,
have gathered in Manhattan
for a fashion show tonight.
Come see the grand creations
by a fabulous designer—
his works are so spectacular!
No clothes were ever finer!
Stepping on the runway first,
a shocking pink carnation.
Next, a purple peony
that's causing a sensation.
Here's a row of daffodils,
dressed in dainty yellow frills,
followed by a hyacinth
wearing blue chiffon.
Now a lily, white as milk,
in a gown of softest silk,
and a pretty poppy
with a proper pantsuit on.

Every blossom
looks so awesome
in the clothing that it wears.
Don't you think
the flowers show us
just how much our Maker cares?

**What fancy dresser could not
outdo the flowers? See Luke 12:27.**

Lunch Line

I fought 'til I got
the very first spot.
I thought that things were fine,
'til Teacher said,
"I think instead,
we'll start at the back of the line."

"Some who seem least important now will be the greatest then."—Luke 13:30

Celestial Celebration

The angels up in Heaven
didn't jump and cheer and shout
every time my soccer team scored.
But boy, did they go bonkers—
they really did rejoice—
the day I gave my heart to the Lord!

What makes the angels happy?
Read Luke 15:10.

99

Loft Teef

"O good grief!
   I loft my upper teef.
      Pleaf helf me find 'em,"
         cried my dear ol' granny.
            I ran and grabbed the broom,
               and we went through every room,
                  where we swept out every
                  little nook and cranny.
               We combed her home
               on all three floors.
               We looked under beds
               as we crawled on all fours.
               We lifted the cushions
               of every last chair,
                  but Granny's lost dentures
                  were simply not there.
               I finally muttered,
               "Let's call it a day,"
               but Granny just glared,
               and she sputtered, "NO WAY."
            "You don't understand,"
            my dear grandmother said.
            "'Til I find my loft teef,
            I will not go to bed.

"I will search through the night
'til I get what I seek.
I will find them all right,
if it takef me all week.
But now if your bedtime.
You muft hit the sack.
I'll get me some rest
when my upperf are back."
The following morning
I woke to the sound
of "Glory to God!
The loft haf been found!"

(Apparently the culprit
was her little kitten, Socks—
he'd buried Granny's choppers
in the kitty litter box.)

**What three stories did Jesus tell about being lost?
See Luke 15.**

Pig Out

Who does this farm hand think he is?
He's eyeing my place at the trough.
He's hoping to make a pig of himself—
he'd better just buzz off!

Will he be a greedy hog
and leave me nothing to eat?
Does he plan to slurp my slop
and gulp up every treat?
My spoiled eggs and dried-up plums,
my melon rinds and bagel crumbs,
my sour grapes and rotten figs—
this fabulous feast fit only for pigs!

Soon the kid will be down on all fours,
chomping my peelings and apple cores,
gobbling my corn cobs and moldy cheese,
gorging himself on my rancid peas.

This lad has a dad in a faraway land
who would gladly pay all his expenses,
if he'd just go home and leave us alone—
oh, why won't he come to his senses?

Read the farmhand's story in Luke 15:11-24.

Party Pooper

The master's son
that ran away
has finally come
back home to stay.

The master cried,
"Oh, this is great!
Let's have a feast
and celebrate!"

But I can't dance,
and I can't laugh.
You see, I am
the fatted calf!

**This poor calf is part of a story Jesus
told in Luke 15:11-24.**

The Father's Heart

He smells like slop and piggy poo.
His clothes are filthy through and through.
But what else can a father do?
I hug him anyway.

His face is caked with dried-up mud.
His lips are cracked and crusted with crud.
But here he stands, my flesh and blood—
I kiss him anyway.

He dirtied up the family name
and then crawled home to me in shame.
But still my heart remains the same—
I love him anyway.

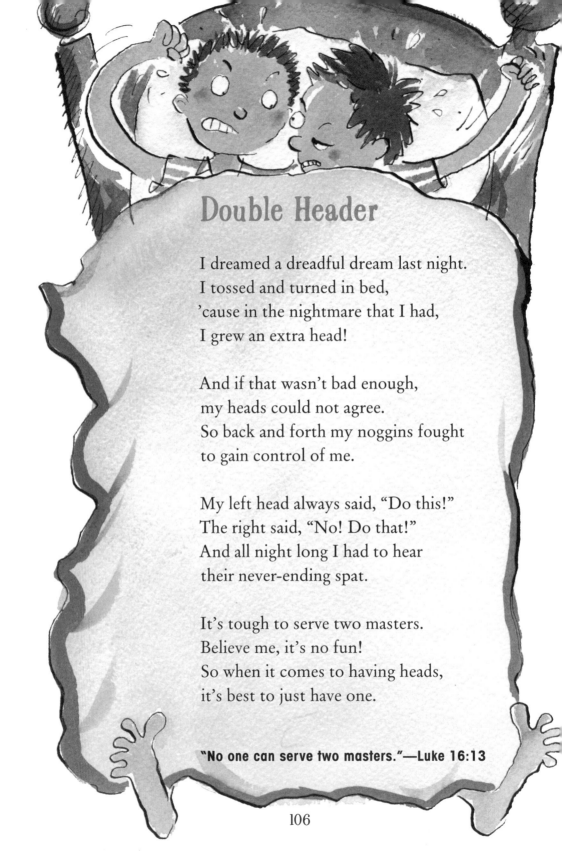

Double Header

I dreamed a dreadful dream last night.
I tossed and turned in bed,
'cause in the nightmare that I had,
I grew an extra head!

And if that wasn't bad enough,
my heads could not agree.
So back and forth my noggins fought
to gain control of me.

My left head always said, "Do this!"
The right said, "No! Do that!"
And all night long I had to hear
their never-ending spat.

It's tough to serve two masters.
Believe me, it's no fun!
So when it comes to having heads,
it's best to just have one.

"No one can serve two masters."—Luke 16:13

Feelings

Where'd you get the notion
Jesus never showed emotion?
Don't forget that he was human too.
He got happy; he got sad.
He got lonely; he got mad.
He had feelings just like me and you.

Jesus loved to laugh out loud
and make a joyful noise.
I bet he got the giggles
when he talked to girls and boys.
And there were times he got upset
with people's stubborn pride.
The Bible says that Jesus wept
when his good friend had died.

So when you talk to Jesus,
it is best to just be real,
'cause Jesus always understands
exactly how you feel.

Then Jesus wept.—John 11:35

Raising a Stink

Phew, Mister Lazarus!
You *reeeaaally* do reek.
You died last Friday,
so it's goin' on a week.

The stench is gettin' stronger,
and it's spreadin' all about.
It's worse than sweaty sneakers
or a pot of sauerkraut.

The scent is bad as any skunk
and makes me plug my nose.
It's grosser than the gooey gunk
that sticks between my toes.

More potent than the odor
that is underneath my arm.
More pungent than the piles
that I step in on the farm.

More vile than the garbage dump,
more sour than the sewer.
More sickening than rotten eggs
or mounds of horse manure.

It is worse than halitosis
or a crowded locker room.
It even has me gagging more
than Grandma's cheap perfume.

It's deadlier than doggie doo
or baby's dirty diaper,
and with each passing minute—
Lazarus is getting riper!

How does this stinkin' story end?
Do things get worse and worse?
Go look up John eleven—
read the forty-fourth verse.

Child Care

Scat! Scram!
Skedaddle! Shoo!
Jesus has no time for you.

What's that, Lord?
What did you say?
You want these little kids to stay?
Shouldn't they run off and play?
Aren't there more important folks
that you must meet today?

Say what, Lord?
Is it true?
Nothing's more important
than these children are to you?

"Let the children come to me."
—Mark 10:14

Needlework

I'd better diet
before I try it.

What's harder than this camel's task?
Read Mark 10:23-25.

True Believer

Father says it isn't feasible.
Mother says it can't be done.
Sister says it's unachievable.
Brother laughs and just pokes fun.
Teacher says it isn't doable.
Cousin says I'm too naive.
But Jesus says all things are possible
for the kid who will believe!

"Everything is possible with God."
—Mark 10:27

Zack, You're Acting Zany!

Zack, you're acting zany!
Zack, this ain't a zoo!
What's a grown-up doing in a tree?
Climbing is for chimps and bears,
for cats and squirrels too—
and yes, of course,
for lively kids like me!

Why was Zacchaeus in that tree?
Read Luke 19:1-10.

114

115

Blind Faith

Blind Bartimaeus,
you're brassy and bold.
Your bellowing is boisterous.
Your barking's uncontrolled.
Your begging bothers Jesus—
please leave the Lord alone.
I've asked you to be quiet.
Now obey what you are told!

Bold Bartimaeus,
your sight is now restored.
Apparently your begging
wasn't bothering the Lord.
For once you were a blind man,
but now at last you see.
(Boy, I bet you're glad
you didn't listen to me!)

**How did Bartimaeus receive his sight?
Read Mark 10:52.**

Pony on Parade?

Why are people shouting
in the streets and on the roofs?
Why are children laying down
their coats before my hoofs?
Why is everybody waving
branches in the air?
Why so much excitement everywhere?

Why would they decide
to have a big parade for me?
Do they think that I have won
some major victory?
Could I be the finest steed
that anyone has seen?
And can you tell me
what exactly does *Hosanna* mean?

I'm just a common donkey,
an ordinary Jack.
I bet the praise
is for the man
who's riding on my back.

Is this donkey right? Look in Luke 19:35-38.

Rock's Role

I'm just your average rock,
and I don't often talk,
'cause rocks don't usually have a lot to say.
But you will want to know
what I witnessed long ago,
one afternoon when Jesus passed my way.

The people formed a crowd,
and they were mighty loud,
singin' out, "Hosanna to the King!"
Then some dudes got so disturbed,
all flustered and perturbed,
and said to Jesus, "Tell 'em not to sing!"

But Jesus just looked down,
and glancin' at the ground,
he pointed to my buddies and to me.
He said, "If folks don't shout,
I'll let these stones cry out,
with songs of praise and shouts of victory."

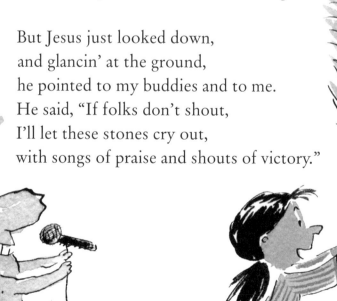

So I've waited in the wings
just in case I need to sing,
if folks like you refuse to do their part.
But it's been two thousand years,
and it certainly appears
that people will keep praisin' him
with all that's in their heart.

No, I do not want to be
a rock star on TV.
I am not pursuing wealth or fame.
But if I could rejoice
and use my gravelly voice,
I'd gladly sing to lift up Jesus' name!

Clearance Sale

Cows mooin'.
Sheep bleatin'.
Doves cooin'.
People meetin'.
Shoppers shoppin'.
Sellers sellin'.
Business hoppin'.
Purses swellin'.
Jesus whippin'.
Peddlers dashin'.
Tables flippin'.
Cages crashin'.
Tills spillin'.
Coins flyin'.
Fences tiltin'.
Lambs cryin'.
Wings flappin'.
Birds escapin'.
Dogs yappin'.
Eyes gapin'.

Did this really happen?
Was Jesus bein' mean?
You can find the truth
in Mark 11:17.

All of Me

I love God with my big muscles,
with my feelings and my brain,
with my red and white corpuscles,
every bone and cell and vein.
I love God with all my talents,
with my smarts and energy,
with the freckles on my face
and every other part of me!

"Love the LORD your God with all your
heart, all your soul, all your mind,
and all your strength."—Mark 12:30

Plink, Plink

Plink, plink,
in the slot.
Two small coins
is all I've got.
Lord, I know
it's not a lot
to put in the
collection pot.

Oh, I wonder
what God thinks
when he hears
the piddly plinks.
Does he say,
"That offering stinks!
Doesn't amount
to diddlysquat!"?
(Look in Mark 12:43
to find what Jesus thought
about the puny offering
this poor old widow brought.)

Use It or Lose It

Don't bury a dollar
down deep in the dirt
and hope that money grows.
I tried it once.
It didn't work—
my dollar decomposed.

Don't bury your talents
down deep in the dirt.
Don't keep them under a lid.
Don't let the gifts
God gave to you
do what my dollar did.

**Read Jesus' story about this in
Matthew 25:14-30.**

Reminders

Sometimes Mama needs reminders
just to jog her memory,
like a string around her finger,
saying, "Don't forget your key."

Sometimes Mama leaves reminders
so that I will not forget,
like a stickie on the fridge:
"Please be sure to feed your pet."

Jesus left me two reminders
of his awesome love for me—
how he gave his blood and body
on the cross at Calvary.

"Do this to remember me."—Luke 22:19

Dried Flowers

Horace and I
were horsin' aroun'
and knocked Mom's favorite
houseplant down.
"Oh, Horace!" I hollered.
"What will we do?
Mom's rare red orchid
is snapped in two!"

"No worries," he said.
"We're in great shape.
Go grab Dad's roll
of gray duct tape."
We stuck the branch
to the longest vine.
In nothin' flat
the plant looked fine . . .

'Til three days later
when our mom found
her beautiful blossoms
all withered and brown.
Horace and I
did extra chores
and bought a new plant
that Mom adores.

(The lesson we learned
should not be ignored—
It's good that we're not
just taped to the Lord.)

"I am the vine; you are the branches."
—John 15:5

129

Fig Twig

I'm just a twig,
not very big.
But I can grow
a juicy fig,
if I will cling
to this ol' limb—
I can't bear fruit
    cut off from him.

    You are a branch
    a lot like me,
    except you have Jesus
    for your tree.

Dream Team

Jesus told us
  to be watchful.
We must stay awake and pray.
C'mon, brothers,
let's be faithful,
    though we've had a busy day.

    James! James!
    Is that you snoring?
    We don't have the time to lose!
  (Yawn.)
John! John!
Are you sleeping?
This is not the time to snoooooozZZZ . . .

**What was Jesus doing
while his friends dozed?
Look in Mark 14:32.**

131

Jesus Got Arrested?

Jesus got arrested?
Oh, heaven forbid!
I thought that he was perfect—
I wonder what he did.

Perhaps he snatched a lady's purse
or pulled a stupid prank.
Maybe he did something worse,
like rob the local bank.

Did he pick a pocket?
Did he start a brawl?
Did he paint graffiti
on the door of city hall?

The Bible says that Jesus
didn't have a single flaw.
So how on earth did Jesus
get all mixed up with the law?

**Why did Jesus get arrested? Look in
Matthew 26:56.**

Early Bird

I am an early riser.
I'm up before the sun.
You see, I am a rooster
with a duty to be done.
It isn't always easy,
and it isn't always fun.
I have to sound the loud alarm
to wake up everyone.

Most people really hate it
when I cock-a-doodle-doo.
They don't appreciate it.
(You would feel the same way too.)

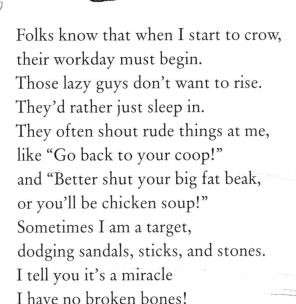

Folks know that when I start to crow,
their workday must begin.
Those lazy guys don't want to rise.
They'd rather just sleep in.
They often shout rude things at me,
like "Go back to your coop!"
and "Better shut your big fat beak,
or you'll be chicken soup!"
Sometimes I am a target,
dodging sandals, sticks, and stones.
I tell you it's a miracle
I have no broken bones!

This morning in the courtyard
as I did my thankless job,
a man named Peter looked at me
and then began to sob.
I know that I'm annoying—
people cover up their ears—
but never has my crowing
brought anyone to tears!

Why did Peter cry? Find out in Matthew 26:69-75.

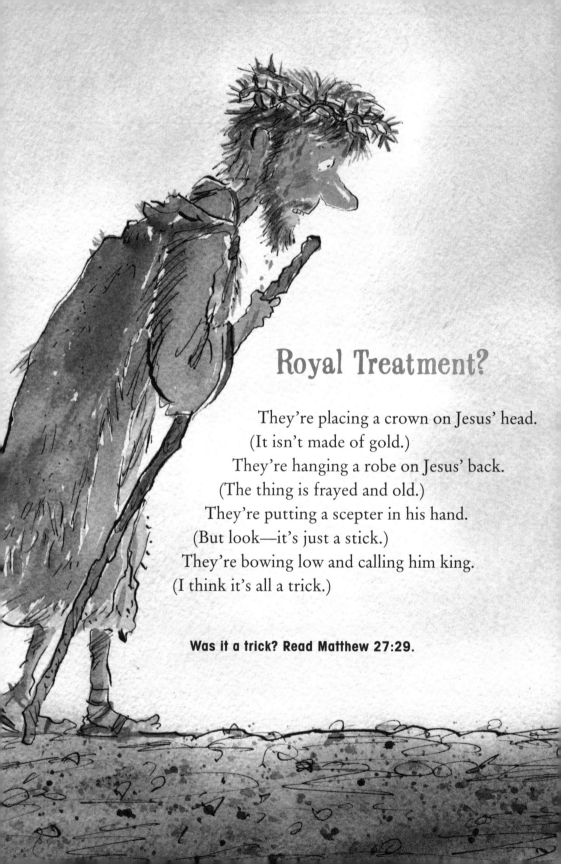

Royal Treatment?

They're placing a crown on Jesus' head.
(It isn't made of gold.)
They're hanging a robe on Jesus' back.
(The thing is frayed and old.)
They're putting a scepter in his hand.
(But look—it's just a stick.)
They're bowing low and calling him king.
(I think it's all a trick.)

Was it a trick? Read Matthew 27:29.

Golgotha

Golgotha is
a gruesome place.
It looks like a skull
with a ghoulish face.
But on that hill
God's showed his grace
and gave his best
to the human race.

Christ Jesus died for us.—Romans 8:34

Open Arms

Today when Dad came home from work,
I met him at the door
and held my arms out, open wide,
like many times before.
I didn't have to speak one word,
since actions say much more.
My daddy knows I love him lots
'cause that's what hugs are for.

When Jesus hung upon the cross,
his arms were open too.
His actions were his way to say,
"I LOVE YOU."

**God showed his great love for us by sending
Christ to die for us.—Romans 5:8**

Good Friday?

I never understood
why we call Good Friday good.
I thought that day
was bad as bad could be.
The Lord was crucified—
    he suffered, bled, and died—
        and that all sounded awfully sad to me.
        But as I thought about it,
        I suddenly could see
        that on that day
        God gave his GOODest
        gift to you and me.

Rolling Stone

I lay three days
at the door of his tomb,
'til early this morning
I heard a big *BOOM!*
An angel said, "Rock,
move away from that hole!
The Lord is alive,
and it's time to roll!"

**Read about this exciting event
in Matthew 28:1-6.**

He's Alive! He's Alive!

He's alive! He's alive!
He is back from the dead!
He rose on the third day,
exactly as he said!

The Lord stood right before me—
what a marvelous surprise!
I saw the Master smile
with my very own eyes!

142

He's alive! He's alive!
So good-bye, I've got to go!
Jesus is alive,
and everybody needs to know!

"I have seen the Lord!"—John 20:18

Page-Turner

Shipwrecks, stonings,
lightning, thunder.
Angels, demons,
signs and wonders.
Noisy riots,
crimes and prisons,
flames of fire,
dreams and visions,
Fortune-tellers,
deadly snakes,
hurricanes and
huge earthquakes.
Healings of the
lame and blind,
miracles of every kind—
WOW!
This book is quite a thriller,
not a bunch of boring facts.
If you love to read adventure,
you will dig the book of Acts.

Home to Heaven

I'm sure that we look silly
and seem a little strange,
just standing here and staring at the sky.
But we just watched the Lord ascend,
then vanish in the clouds—
    you see, it's sort of sad to say good-bye.

But Jesus made a promise—
    his words were very clear.
    He said he wouldn't leave us high and dry.
    But soon he'd send his Spirit
    to live with us down here
    and fill us with his power from on high.

Jesus will come again! Read Acts 1:11.

The Holy Spirit Comes

All of us were startled
by a sudden whooshing sound.
We thought a mighty hurricane
was blowing through our town!
Then fire rested on our heads,
but not a hair was burned.
We praised the Lord in languages
that we had never learned!
Our leader, Peter, stood and then
began to preach the Word.
His sermon stirred our hearts and souls
as everybody heard
how Jesus Christ was crucified
to take away our sin.
Three thousand people turned to God,
and they were born again!

God sent his Holy Spirit
with a powerful outpouring.
The very first service of his new church
was anything but boring!

Read this exciting story in Acts 2.

Better Than Silver or Gold

I can walk!
I can run!
I can leap and dance!
I can race and march
and pace and prance!
I amble and scramble and ramble and romp!
I scurry and scuffle and scamper and stomp!
I skip! I sprint! Just look at me go!
I dash and dart and do-se-do!
I bolt and bounce; I boogie and bop!
I jog and jive; I hustle and hop!

Watch me now!
I'll cut a rug
with an Irish jig or the jitterbug.
I'll cartwheel on the neighbor's lawn.
I'll run the Boston Marathon.
You know, I could go on and on . . .

I just thank God for Peter and John!

**"In the name of Jesus Christ the Nazarene,
get up and walk!"—Acts 3:6**

Wake-Up Call

Christians make me crazy.
They cause my skin to crawl.
All their talk of Jesus
really drives me up the wall!
They're nothin' but fanatics.
Their brains are weak and small.
I feel it is my duty
to eradicate them all.
I'm traveling to Damascus.
I'm feeling proud and tall.
Can't wait to give those Christians
a shocking wake-up call.

CRACK!
A blinding flash of light!
Look out, I'm gonna fall!
Ow! My body's aching
as I lay here in a sprawl.
Everywhere is darkness.
I cannot see at all.
I hear a voice from Heaven—
it's calling to me,
"SAUL!"

To be continued. See Acts 9.

B-B-But L-Lord . . .

Oh Lord, my knees are knockin'.
I'm sweatin' and I'm shakin'.
You're sure that I should go
and pray for Saul?
    You say he's changed his thinkin',
    but what if he is fakin'?
        He's known for killin' Christians, after all.

You say to lay my hands on him
    and pray that he will see,
        but what if Saul decides instead
        to lay his hands on me?!

All right, OK, I will obey.
    I'll do exactly as you say.
        Forgive me, Lord, for tryin' to save my skin.
        But if I'm not back home by three,
            please do this one last thing for me,
                and kindly go inform my next of kin.

Who was this nervous messenger?
Read Acts 9:10.

The Great Escape

Peter the apostle
made the perfect prison break,
with more suspense than any flick
that Hollywood could make.
He didn't use a file
someone baked into a cake.
He found no hidden key
or secret tunnel he could take.

So how did Peter pull it off?
How did it come about?
Acts chapter 12 will tell you how
this jailbird busted out!

Jailhouse Rock

Silas and I were sittin' in a cell,
dark and dank with a moldy old smell.
Silas and I could easily tell
our work for God wasn't goin' so well.

Our feet were in fetters and fastened to a chain.
Our wrists were in shackles; our bodies were in pain.
Sure looked like our ministry was goin' down the drain.
Couldn't be a better time to grumble and complain!

Instead, I said to Silas, "Why mumble and moan?
What good does it do if we gripe and we groan?
We may be in prison, but our God is on the throne!
His Spirit lives within us, so we know we're not alone."

I opened up my mouth, and I belted out a song,
and soon brother Silas was a-singin' right along.
We knew by praisin' Jesus we just couldn't go wrong!
Our hearts were encouraged, and our hope grew strong.

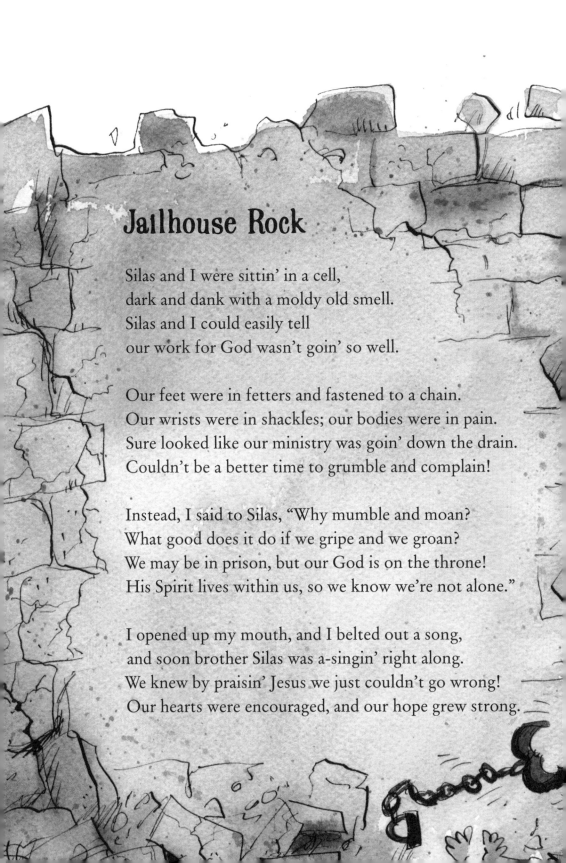

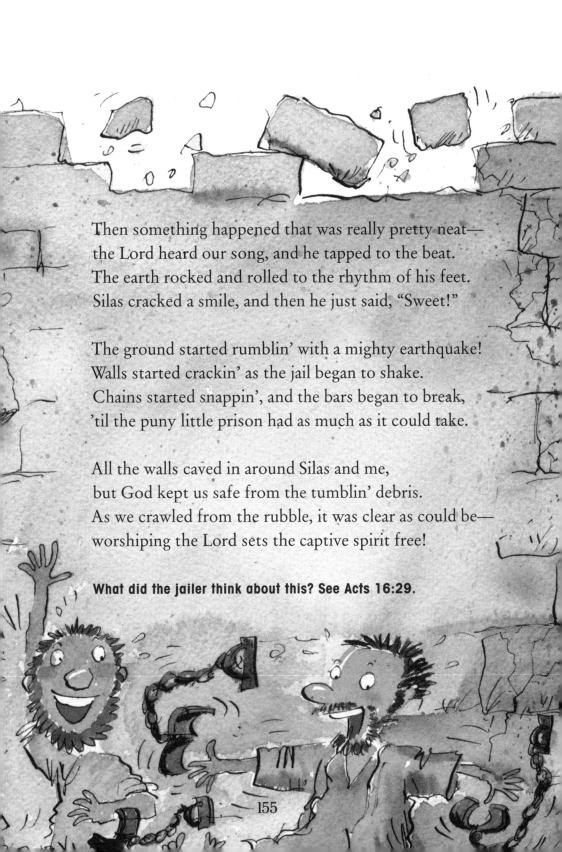

Then something happened that was really pretty neat—
the Lord heard our song, and he tapped to the beat.
The earth rocked and rolled to the rhythm of his feet.
Silas cracked a smile, and then he just said, "Sweet!"

The ground started rumblin' with a mighty earthquake!
Walls started crackin' as the jail began to shake.
Chains started snappin', and the bars began to break,
'til the puny little prison had as much as it could take.

All the walls caved in around Silas and me,
but God kept us safe from the tumblin' debris.
As we crawled from the rubble, it was clear as could be—
worshiping the Lord sets the captive spirit free!

What did the jailer think about this? See Acts 16:29.

Dead Tired

Hello, my name is Eutychus,
and I did something ludicrous,
long ago when I was just a kid.
You wanna know the facts?
Go check the book of Acts,
'cause chapter 20 tells you what I did.

(But here's a hint for those of you
who fall asleep in church—
you'd better be particular
when choosing where to perch.)

Peter and Paul

Peter and Paul were important apostles
      who penned some epistles you've possibly read.
Or were they epistles who wrote the apostles?
      Ooh, now it's all criss-crossled up in my head!

Mixed Blessing

I wouldn't wanna eat four cups of flour—
my mouth would get all powdery and dry.
I wouldn't wanna eat three cups of sugar—
I'd feel so sick that I would wanna die.
I wouldn't eat a spoon of baking soda—
My belly would get bubbly and bloat.
I wouldn't drink a teaspoon of vanilla—
I'd sputter as it trickled down my throat.
I wouldn't wanna swallow down a slimy raw egg—
I know that I would gag if I did that!
And surely I would shudder if I ate a stick of butter,
'cause it's nothing but a quarter pound of fat!

But if I stir this stuff up all together,
it starts to look delicious, as you know,
and suddenly it tastes a whole lot better,
'cause now it is a batch of cookie dough!
Ingredients aren't great all by their lonesome—
you know that I would eat 'em if I could—
but somehow all these things do work together,
and *YUM!*—they work together for my good!

**In all things God works for the good of those who
love him.—Romans 8:28, NIV**

Strong Attachment

God makes a gooey glue.
It's supersticky stuff.
It's strong and indestructible.
It's durable and tough.
Nothing in creation
can dissolve God's superglue.
It's what he uses
when he glues his
love to me and you!

**Nothing can ever separate us from God's love.
—Romans 8:38**

God's House

My body isn't built with lumber,
concrete, plaster, glass, or bricks.
My body isn't made with marble,
stone or stucco, steel or sticks.

My body has no roof or steeple,
windows, ceiling, doors, or dome.
Still my body is a temple—
it's the Holy Spirit's home.

**Your body is the temple of
the Holy Spirit.**
—1 Corinthians 6:19

Body Functions

I wouldn't be a very good ear—
I can't hear.

I wouldn't be a very good eye—
I can't cry.

I don't breathe air,
I don't pump blood,

so I would be
a lousy lung or heart.

You'd only complain
if I were your brain,
'cause I just ain't that smart.

But where would you be
if you didn't have me
to help with your digestin'?
So we are agreed
you certainly need—
me, your small intestine!

God has given us different gifts for doing certain things well.—Romans 12:6

The Eagle, the Beagle, and the Seagull

"I wish I were an eagle," said the beagle.
"It must be nice to fly up high
 and live so wild and free."

"I wish I were a beagle," said the seagull.
"I bet it's fun to run and chase
 a squirrel up a tree."

"I wish I were a seagull," said the eagle.
"Then I could sit and eat my fish
 while floating on the sea."

And so all three
of these unhappy creatures
just sat around and dreamed about
who they would rather be.

Grace

We have a springer spaniel pup.
We chose to name her Grace.
She has a cute expression
on her sweet, angelic face.

But looks can be deceiving,
for she's such a naughty pup!
She makes a lot of messes—
you can guess who cleans 'em up.

She chews and chews on Daddy's shoes.
She shreds up every lace.
Her sloppy, floppy puppy paws
broke Momma's favorite vase.

She dirties up the furniture
with soggy doggie drool.
She even got suspended
from her puppy training school.

Our dog is still a youngster,
so she needs some growing space.
Her name is a reminder
we must give her lots of
GRACE.

God gives us his grace too. Read Ephesians 2:8.

Fruit Bowl

I wrote *Love* on a plastic banana
and *Joy* on a plastic pear.
I printed *Peace* on a plastic peach
with great artistic flair.

Patience I scrawled on an apple.
Kindness I squeezed on a grape.
Goodness I scratched on an apricot.
My fruit bowl was taking shape.

Faithfulness I scribbled on a kiwi.
Gentleness I jotted on a plum.
Self-control I put on an orange.
My fruit bowl was finally done.

It sits on the dining room table,
so now when I go near it,
I'm quickly reminded my life should produce
the fruit of the Holy Spirit.

Find the Holy Spirit's fruit in Galatians 5:22, 23.

Extended Family

My family's sort of smallish.
It's just my mom and me.
But though there's only two of us,
we're still a family.

Our family could get bigger,
though we'll have to wait and see.
Momma might get married,
and then we'd grow to three.

But if this never happens,
still my mom and I agree,
that we will always be a part
of God's *big* family!

You are members of God's family.
—Ephesians 2:19

Wilma Worrisome

My name is Wilma Worrisome.
I worry night and day.
I keep so busy fretting
that I have no time to pray.
I wring my hands and chew my nails,
because I'm so uptight.
I pace the floor and get cold sweats.
I toss and turn all night.
People often say to me,
"Why don't you just chill out?"
But there are many urgent things
to get worked up about—

Will all the stars stay in the sky?
Will mountains disappear?
Will August come before July
or be postponed this year?
Will the cacti beat the heat?
Will the penguins get cold feet?
Will possums wait to cross the street
until the coast is clear?

Help!

I'm sure you see how God needs me
to stew and fuss and care.
He understands I'm just too stressed
to go to him in prayer.

Learn what to do instead of worrying.
Read Philippians 4:6.

Can-Do Attitude

I have a good friend, Gabriel.
He is the coolest dude.
He has a fearless spirit
and a can-do attitude.
Though Gabe has disabilities,
they do not slow him down.
The guy has all the energy
of any kid around.

My buddy's on a baseball team.
He hit a big home run.
He is a whiz at video games
and trounces everyone.
He plays percussion in the band—
the snare drum, like a pro.
And riding on his scooter,
Gabe is always on the go.

He wrestles with his brother
and goes skiing with his dad.
He does his chores and schoolwork
(which makes his mother glad).

My friend was born in April.
He arrived the thirteenth day.
He celebrates on 4-13,
I guess that you could say.
Gabe's got a favorite Bible verse
(his birthday gives a clue).
Go find it in Philippians—
Gabe thinks you'll like it too!

**Who gives Gabe strength? Read Gabe's
favorite verse to find out.**

Every Day's Thanksgiving

There is a lot
I'm thankful for today,
but this is just the twenty-first of May—
Thanksgiving is a half a year away.
So how will I remember,
if I wait until November,
all the words of thanks
that I would like to say?

(I think I'll just be thankful every day!)

Be thankful in all circumstances.
—1 Thessalonians 5:18

Let's eat hamburgers!

A Good Example

My mama often says to me,
"Now set a good example
for your little baby sister, Peggy Sue."
But though I'm only ten,
I know that now and then
the grown-ups need a good example too!

How can you be an example? Read 1 Timothy 4:12.

Bodyguards

The angels that watch over me
are not the wimpy kind,
those chubby ones with baby wings
we glue on valentines.
My angels have big biceps!
They're muscular and strong.
They guard me while I sleep at night
They're with me all day long.

They're buffer than the blockers
for the Packers or the Bears.
They're tougher than the tacklers
for the Broncs or Buccaneers.
They're burly and they're brawny—
they're as brave as brave can be.
So bullies, don't you bother
comin' 'round to mess with me!

What do angels do?
Read Hebrews 1:14 to find out.

My Conscience

God gave me a gift called a conscience.
It works like a wee little voice.
It whispers to me what's right and wrong
when I must make a choice.

God gave me a gift called a conscience.
I'll keep it uncluttered and clear,
so I can be tuned to God's Spirit
whenever he speaks in my ear.

God can fix a guilty conscience.
Look in Hebrews 10:22.

Tough to Tame

Lions and tigers and bears? Oh, please—
any ol' trainer can tame them with ease.
Elephants, dolphins, and chimpanzees?
Teaching these creatures is truly a breeze.

But *I* have a whole crew of trained wallabies
who check that my car has enough antifreeze.
I taught a macaw how to make mac and cheese
and shout out "Gesundheit!" whenever I sneeze.

My poodle, my pug, and my sweet Pekingese,
my calico cat, and my sleek Siamese
have more than impeccably fine pedigrees—
all of my pets have earned college degrees.

My parrot knows more than the mere ABCs.
That bird can quote Shakespeare in French and Chinese.
My horse can, of course, count by fours or by threes,
but nuclear physics is his expertise.

I also train kids like mean Mona McPhees
to always say "May I?" and "Thank you" and "Please."
I finally got finicky Freddy Ortiz
to love to eat broccoli, carrots, and peas!

But there is one thing with a sting like a bee's
I've found to be tougher to tame than all these.
A look at James 3:8 and one quickly sees
that even the Bible completely agrees!

Dull Roar

The devil's like a lion.
He loves to rant and roar.
His ruckus can be raucous,
and it's tough to just ignore.
But when he tries
to tell me lies
and fill my heart with fear,
I boldly lift my voice and say,
"Hey, Devil, listen here!
I am not afraid of your gummy ol' jaws.
I am not afraid of your fluffy little paws.
Jesus lives inside of me
and I'm a child of God.
And Devil, you're defeated,
you're defanged,
and you're declawed."

Resist the devil, and he will flee from you.
—James 4:7

Squeaky Clean

I love nothing better
than a big ol' bubble bath,
to sit and soak 'til I am squeaky clean.
I gather up the lather,
and I wash my face and toes
and all the other places in-between.

Soap can only scrub me on the outside.
It's great for getting grimies off my skin.
But when it comes to cleaning up the inside,
nothing but the blood of Christ
can wash away my sin!

Never Too Old

Great-great-grandma's ninety-seven.
Great-great-grandpa's ninety-nine.
But when God looks down from Heaven,
he still says, "They're kids of mine."

We are children of God.
—1 John 5:19

Lukewarm

No one likes a lukewarm cup of cocoa.
A lukewarm baked potato ain't so hot.
No one likes a lukewarm bowl of chili.
We prefer it steaming from the pot.

No one likes a lukewarm ice cream sundae.
Lukewarm lemonade just isn't cool.
No one likes a thermos full of lukewarm milk
packed inside the lunch we take to school.

Jesus said we cannot be halfhearted.
We must choose if we'll be cold or hot.
Who would want to be a wimpy, lukewarm kid?
Let's serve the Lord with everything we've got!

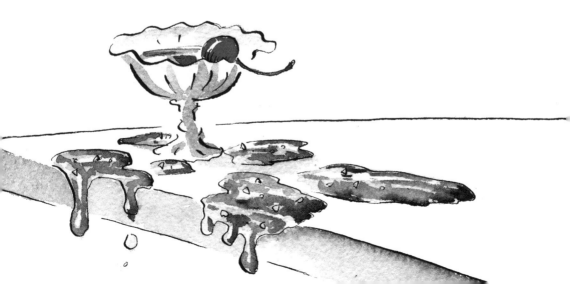

No Comparison

I've heard people say,
"It is heaven on earth!"
as they try to describe
a delicious dessert.
Then I read in the Book
what it looks like up there,
and I know nothing here
can begin to compare.

What does Heaven look like?
Read Revelation 21:9-27.

On Monday I Was Moody

On Monday I was moody.
On Tuesday I was tense.
On Wednesday I felt wonderful
and full of confidence.
On Thursday I was truly thrilled,
but Friday I freaked out.
By Saturday I felt so sad,
I only moped about.

Our lesson Sunday morning
was Hebrews 13:8.
We learned that Jesus stays the same
no matter what the date.
I'm glad that Jesus doesn't change
with every little whim.
I'm gonna pray that I might be
a whole lot more like him.

**Jesus Christ is the same yesterday,
today, and forever.—Hebrews 13:8**

Subject Index

Page numbers refer to pages where poems begin.

Scripture Index

Page numbers refer to pages where poems begin.